GREN

25 brief studies of the cu   , combative and
corrupted

Thomas McColl

First published 2020 by Fly on the Wall Press

Published in the UK by

Fly on the Wall Press

56 High Lea Rd

New Mills

Derbyshire

SK22 3DP

www.flyonthewallpoetry.co.uk

ISBN: 978-1-913211-13-4

Typesetting and Cover Design by Isabelle Kenyon. Cover photo public domain work from Unsplash.

Supported using public funding by

ARTS COUNCIL ENGLAND

LOTTERY FUNDED

On 'Grenade Genie':

"When I first read these poems I knew I was in the presence of a real poet writing honestly and perceptively, exploring what it means to be alive in these unsettling times. He takes poetry seriously but never himself and indeed some poems make you explode with laughter."

- Rodney Wood, Poet

"It could be London, or any major city. Thomas McColl writes about a wasteland more frightening than Eliot's, but one where you still have to laugh at the craziness. A world of Instagram, security passes and decaying nuclear bunkers, where millions are spewed in and out of the Underground while being bombarded by invitations to go shopping. Where it isn't even safe to cross the road, and what happened to the trees? This is very definitely a book of poems for our times."

- Merryn Williams, Bloodaxe Poet and Critic

"In 'Grenade Genie' Tom McColl goes urban exploring on our behalf. In the half-light he roams the plains of London and goes shopping with Greek heroes, mining the underground and bringing up the bodies to the surface so we can identify them. Absurd flights of fantasy and too real memories are observed via the relentless gaze of the digital. These poems are not snapshots. They are long exposures of life, he sees us, and he sees himself, with a brilliant clarity."

- Barry Fentiman-Hall, Poet

" 'Grenade Genie' is a collection that is well needed in these uncertain times, where political and social issues fill our pages. This is a must read where political poetry should be read and heard. I do highly recommend this book to anyone interested in the current contemporary poetry scene; the book comes as twenty-five brief studies of the cursed, coerced, combative and corrupted. The urgency in these pages needs to be heard today."

- **Matt Duggan, Poet**

Contents

Cursed

Coerced

Combative

Corrupted

Previous Publications

The Evil Eye *International Times*

Carry My Eyes (Above and Across the Barbed-wire Border) *Refugees Welcome: Poems in a Time of Crisis (Eyewear)*

The Bunker *Poems for Grenfell Tower (The Onslaught Press)*

All the Beach is a Stage *Runcible Spoon*

The Greatest Poem *Queen Mob's Tea House*

Security Pass *DNA Magazine*

Lightning Strikes *Co-Incidental 4 (The Black Light Engine Room Press)*

Invisible Twin *The High Window*

Nightclubbing in Brum, 1988 *Arts Foundry*

Jan, Jen or Jean *Psychopoetica*

Shopping with Perseus *Geeked*

Socialist Workers on Oxford Street *Co-Incidental 4 (The Black Light Engine Room Press)*

Statement by the Pedestrian Liberation... *I am not a Silent Poet*

Obsolete *Paper & Ink*

The Phoney War *Atrium*

It was a Cut-up *Hot Tub Astronaut*

Hooked *Burning House Press Online*

The Surgery I go to has a two-headed doctor *Poems for the NHS at 70 (The Onslaught Press)*

First Kiss *Burning House Press Online*

Literal Library *The Journal*

CURSED

NO LONGER QUITE SO SURE

The council is yet to cut back
the branches of the trees on Newman Road,
which means that, halfway through
my journey to work on the bus –
and always just as I fall asleep
in my usual seat on the upper deck,
with my hooded head at rest against the glass –
the low-hanging branches attack me in the dream I'm having.
And I'm caught out every time for I'm always so tired –
and, in any event, I guess I'm helpless,
being one of those hundreds of thousands of people
always letting themselves be eaten and then spewed out
by any one of hundreds of number-branded hairless bison
that charge across the city in all directions every day.

We are all living lives more and more unnatural,
and in this messed-up world,
where buses are bison and people are grass,
it's no longer shocking to find
that glass is air and branches are blades.
At any rate, what happens each time is that
the jutting branches the bison headbutts

immediately return to wreak revenge

and, on giving my window the coarsest caress,

invade the dream I'm having

like they're the bladed fingers of Freddie Krueger,

scoring my brain,

and in shock – but just in time – I wake up,

my brain unbloodied but my mind unhinged.

Today is no exception:

I'm violently awoken

but, this time round, just after it's happened,

and I glance at the section of window

where my head's been resting,

I notice a message etched in the glass –

We're gonna take the city back –

which, in the past, I'd have automatically assumed

was done by some school kid,

by locker key or compass from his pencil case,

but now – as the bus passes the derelict factory on Leonard Street,

and I can see that, already, poking through the smashed windows

are branches of small trees – I'm no longer quite so sure.

THE EVIL EYE

You're too far gone,
and clearly unable to heed my plea –
but still I have to tell you, son:
You wouldn't expect a key
to leave its shadow behind
when picked up from a table,
but that's what's happening now to you, online.

Hidden interests constantly mine your data –
every moment you're manipulated –
but as long as your need to exist
(like everyone else now needs to exist)
is sated, everything's fine.

And, let's face it, how can you stop?
It's fame, albeit the tiniest drop –
even if there's no-one
who could possibly give a damn
about these selfies you constantly upload
on to Facebook, Twitter and Instagram.

Don't you realise
that you exist no more than you did before –
less, in fact?
You've made a pact with the digital devil,
not even to be an insect preserved in amber,
but simply an insect that's landed on a cobweb
stretched out directly in front of an amber signal
and as soon as you're lit up, no-one hangs around.

You've allowed yourself to get caught in a cobweb
spun by a social spider that sucks you dry of information,
then leaves your hollowed-out exoskeletal frame
to rot on its website.

In any event, the next day, there's a brand-new cobweb;
once again you feel the need to be captured.

Reality – which, after all, is the resin of reason –
dictates that, even with your endless selfies,
your life is no more or less preserved
than the totally unrecorded life of the Afghan shepherd
who, in 1971, believing (correctly)
the camera lens to be the evil eye,
refused to allow a hapless hippy to take his photograph.

Knowing his soul would be sucked dry –

and that whatever he did

(whether he acquiesced or not),

the hindered hippy's straightened-out son

would be back for Queen and Country

in thirty years' time –

the shepherd pointed the barrel of his rifle

straight at the horrified hippy's acid-drenched head

and told him to *get the fuck out of Helmand*.

You're too far gone,

and clearly unable to heed my plea –

but still I have to tell you, son:

Just because there's no going back to the 7th century,

doesn't mean there's nothing you can learn

from its doomed last stand against the present one.

CARRY MY EYES (ABOVE AND ACROSS THE BARBED-WIRE BORDER)

The best I can do, by daylight,

hiding in the undergrowth beyond the camp,

is fall asleep and let eyelids, turned into wings, carry my eyes

(in my dreams, always the colour of sky-high blue)

above and across the barbed-wire border.

I'm awoken when my eyes return

and burn into me the realisation

that, even if I don't drown in the peat bogs

or get taken down by the prowling guards

with their vicious dogs,

getting across is no guarantee of success.

Europe – which projects a gorgon-frenzied lust for freedom

(that turns to stone as soon as it knows

it's captured you in its flat-line eyebrowed trance) –

is a never-ending fortress.

Whoever said the modern world was round

has never seen its medieval edge here at the borderline.

No Twitter post can compete with a border post:

Millions of messages lie out of sight,

obscured by one unwelcoming sign.

I hear that there are many now discussing our terrible plight,

saying *welcome the refugee*,

but my tear-tortured eyes are tired

of earning nothing more than sympathy.

I return to the crowded squalid camp

and exhausted, again fall asleep.

This time, as they fly across the border,

my dreaming-of-a-new-life blood-shot eyes

spy the approach of reporters in roving bands.

We're here to tell your story, they always say,

how you fled civil war and want to be given a chance.

But I know that they don't care –

they'll turn my truth into some kind of lie,

and I won't talk to them, nor extend my palm

(which would reveal my cut and calloused lifeline),

just tell them with a steely stare:

Don't hug me with your inverted commas,

nor touch me with your cruel chameleon hands.

THE BUNKER

Our seedy tower block
sits on top of a Cold War nuclear bunker,
both the work of cowboy builders
who all died in mysterious circumstances,
one by one, throughout the 1970s.
Even now, after years of demanding answers,
no-one's prepared to address our concerns –
and all because they concern a structure
which still, officially, doesn't exist.

I wasn't alive in 1965
when the Ministry of Secret Buildings,
continuing to keep the bunker's location secret,
failed to inform the Ministry of Misconceived Ideas,
which allowed our high-rise flats to be built on top.

I was very much alive though in 1991
when I inadvertently discovered
the bunker's entrance late one evening.
Hearing cries for help in dense shrubs near our block,
I found a loose manhole cover
and, descending a rusty ladder

into a sprawling concrete complex,

was shocked to stumble upon charred human remains.

Terrified, I ran straight out and rang the police,

but after bundling me into their car

the plain clothes slipped acid into my tea at the station;

charged me with possession

and making a false report whilst under the influence.

By the time the charges were dropped,

the 'cash-strapped' council had hurriedly built a basketball court

at the very spot where the manhole cover had been.

Well, here I am, just about alive in 2017.

Hard experience has made me realise

what we, as residents, are up against,

but the bunker – a ticking time bomb – remains beneath us,

and though that acid trip might have clouded my memory

and maybe the bunker never was filled up with burnt bodies,

it still needs to be condemned, along with our block –

two Cold War relics that have no place in the 21st Century.

And it's not just me: most residents have come to realise

the government's trying to hide an omen.

Let's face it: every time they claim there's nothing there,

but won't explain why that information is 'classified',

it's clear the bunker does exist;

I wasn't off my head.

Meanwhile, fearing a cover-up,

residents worry that this shoddily-built structure we inhabit,

undermined by the crumbling bunker,

will eventually collapse.

But I know what I saw and, even if it was all just in my mind,

it portends a fate that's even worse:

what the bunker was never used for

may someday be unleashed, a stored-up curse,

as destructive as a nuclear blast,

but more concentrated,

spiralling as a furious fire,

then collapsing catastrophically

into black holes

that once were windows.

ALL THE BEACH IS A STAGE

The stuck-in-the-silent-era Moon

(which, tonight, full-faced, is able again to play the part

of the shining star – though never actually gets to be one)

is, with its hemispherical floodlight, ensuring that all the beach is

a stage...

...which makes it unfortunate then that, way down here,

on this theatrically-moonstruck night,

the vast stage of sand remains a desert, devoid of drama.

Even so – and despite there being no audience to speak of –

the show must go on, for the one and only act:

a hi-vis yellow-jacketed middle-aged man and his long-suffering

assistant,

a low-vis multi-faceted metal detector –

the only hope this duo has of ever getting rich.

Not that that's actually saying much,

when the metal detector's head – as flat as the Earth once was

and programmed simply to dream of Martial's money –

is certainly never going to make its one and only dream come true,

as neither the Moon nor Neptune

will give up their sunken Roman fortune

but instead offer up, each time,

a fool's flotsam of faded junk and seagulls' bones.

The dupondius-dreaming duo, though, refuse to give up hope –

or, at least, the one hungriest for fame and riches

is trying his best to stay upbeat.

While gripping a lit cigar-sized torch between his teeth –

in lieu of the finest Cuban he'll one day buy –

this paltry-paid performer remains convinced

it's only time before he stumbles upon his fortune here.

It cannot be that life's a beach and then you die –

even if his two-bit two-part act is decidedly end-of-pier.

First up, in the torch's unforgiving spotlight,

the dull black disk appears,

doing, as ever, its best impression of a dolphin.

Not bad, and vaguely amusing,

but still a one-trick pony (or, even worse, a no-trick dolphin).

So, the disappointing disk disappears,

only for an equally dull black boot to swiftly take its place in the spotlight,

doing, as it always does, a quick and pointless dance,

a five second shuffle, shifting sand,

just to find – and as it will be ever thus –

that no-one's getting paid.

THE GREATEST POEM

I've been thinking,

that if I visit the Nayland Rock Shelter

overlooking Margate Sands

at the right time in the autumn of 2021 –

exactly 100 years on

from when Thomas Stearns Eliot went there

to write his masterpiece, *The Waste Land*,

the greatest poem of the 20th Century –

then, if I sit there long enough with my laptop,

maybe I'll end up writing

the greatest poem of the 21st Century.

Things in my favour:

My first name is Thomas,

I once worked for Lloyds Bank,

and I write poetry.

Things that might go against me:

My surname isn't Eliot, it's McColl,

working for Lloyds Bank

is, in itself, no indicator of literary talent,

and, anyway, history doesn't tend to repeat itself.

In fact, what if, this time round, the inverse happens,
and I end up writing the worst poem of the 21ˢᵗ Century?

In the current climate, it's highly likely.
Let's face it – Thomas Sterns Eliot
had advances in psychoanalysis
to help him get in the right frame of mind…

…whereas all I have is advances in social media.
Who knows? Maybe, by 2021,
I'll have no choice but to fit my opus
into four lines on Instagram.

But then, when I do,
my simple, artless platitude
will inexplicably receive a million likes,
and then, released as part of a book,
will inexplicably sell a million copies,
and my poem will be so bad
that everyone will definitely remember it much more
than whatever the best poem of the 21ˢᵗ Century
will actually be – written, perhaps,
by someone who, like Eliot,
may be going through difficult times,

and talented enough to harness adversity,

will, out of that, create a brilliant, epic poem,

but, unfortunately, there'll no longer be anyone

with the attention span to read it,

let alone publish it,

and he or she, in despair, will delete it

and give up writing altogether…

…whereas I'll go on to publish book after book,

and William McGonagall will turn in his grave

at no longer being the worst poet in the English language,

usurped by Thomas McColl…

…now famous for having written

the worst poem of the 21st Century,

or indeed any century,

but that's the thing – writing the worst ever poem

is no barrier anymore to immense success.

Thomas Sterns Eliot may well have been the best,

but there's no room for that now.

Now, it has to be four lines or less,

and totally trite:

1921 –

been and gone.

2021 –

bring it on.

GRENADE GENIE

Possessing genius is one thing,

but are you prepared,

on finding it encased inside a grenade,

to pull out the pin to release the genie,

and therefore be

on the receiving end of the huge explosion?

In other words, are you prepared to be obliterated –

meaning you won't even get to see,

above the billowing smoke,

the now-released genie granting every wish

to all your atoms that, dispersed,

and already forming into new but lesser versions of you,

will proceed to take all the credit you were due

as if you'd never actually existed,

as if the credit had always been theirs to take?

Essentially, it's genius for everyone else's sake but yours,

yet still the only kind of genius worth possessing –

the kind that changes everything:

Grenade-less genius is worthless.

It's just that, if it turns out you're the one who pulls the pin,

there's no guarantee you'll even be remembered,

for only one thing is certain:

The grenade genie –

arbiter of atoms –

doesn't care.

He knows that genius is a combustible commodity;

once released,

he's simply there to give out

all the credit indiscriminately.

Anyway, the undeserving horde

that ends up in receipt of it

will, soon enough, be wiped out too,

when everyone least expects it,

in the unlikeliest place –

and it's almost always

the unlikeliest person who'll set things off.

So, who knows, maybe it will be you:

out of luck and living in abject poverty,

with nothing to lose –

your possession of genius amounting to nothing more

than the pulled pin held between your teeth,

and the self-belief that got you there…

…except that there, as it turns out,
is right in the middle of nowhere.
But that's fate, and though the explosion will mean
your life ending without you being, in any way, rewarded,
the main thing is that history will be made —
and incredibly:
vast armies of advancing traditionalists
(who seemed, to everyone, unstoppable)
all taken out with just one genius-filled grenade.

And who knows? Maybe the day will come
when the atoms you released upon your death
(which, having congealed into lesser versions of you,
the genie bestowed all credit upon)
will, in gratitude, honour your selfless act
by placing, at the very spot
where you blew yourself up,
a commemorative plaque
as round and blue as the Earth…

…the Earth, which, in billions of years,
the Sun will swallow up.

And that's the thing (why none of it really matters):

even the round, blue Earth –

along with your round, blue plaque –

must one day shatter into atoms too.

Let's face it,

everything and everyone

is nothing more than atoms

Even the brightest human is nothing more

than the lowliest animal, organism

or inanimate object:

it doesn't take a genius to work that out.

And though nothing matters

when we're all just matter,

it still remains

that people who think

they're more than what they're made of

are there to be brought down.

Even if that moment's unplanned,

the grenade genie –

arbiter of atoms –

will always be on hand.

Trust me, somewhere, right at this very moment –

a moment borne out of desperation –

there's another rat amongst the dinosaurs

about to pull out the pin with its teeth.

COERCED

SECURITY PASS

I've just been made permanent –
yet already I know I'm completely expendable.

In any event, I've today, at last, received a 'full' security pass.
It comes complete with a freshly taken photograph,
my face displaying a grimace that was nothing more
than confused surprise at the sudden camera flash,
an expression that could almost pass
for a desperate act of brave defiance,
though no-one's fooled and no-one cares.

Anyway, the doors opening in this building
aren't opening for me but for the magnetic stripe across the card.
I know full well already that it's numbers on a line,
not the letters in my name, the system recognises –
that a thin row of binary
will always trump any last shred of humanity.

Let's face it, though now clearly displayed in **bold**,
my name, Thomas McColl, remains completely incidental,
as impotent as a name that just about belongs still
to some hitherto proud family firm –

which, having been swallowed up by a vast conglomerating entity,

is slowly but surely stripped of its former identity,

until there's nothing left but the name itself

(a name that's only being kept in place

to satisfy some irritating legal obligation).

Thomas McColl Limited.

That's me: Limited — extremely limited —

a lowly worker whose pass gives him access

to just one floor in a forty-two-floor building.

Well, here I am, on the forty-first floor.

As soon as I exit the lift,

directly in front of me, the main door,

and there, above it, the clocking-in-and-out security camera,

an irritating creature which is probably related,

in some way, to the camera that took

the annoyingly crappy picture displayed on my pass.

Then, catching my reflection in the door's dark glass —

an expression that could almost pass

for a desperate act of brave defiance —

I realise, in a flash, that my mug, in fact, has now been set to project

a permanent stamped-on-the-face look of confused compliance, and that my brand-new pass doesn't represent me,

but that I simply represent my brand-new pass.

LIGHTNING STRIKES

Lightning strikes the letter D in company sign outside HQ,
which falls and kills the passing Chairman instantly.

Bits of brain containing next year's business plan
are instantaneously passed on to his deputy,
who's reportedly in a terrible state,
his Armani suit now ruined completely
(though a wholly undeserved but expected promotion –
plus hefty bonus – should compensate).

At any rate,
not even nature's dramatic intervention
can help workers at the plant.
A few days later –
brought to their knees before the brand-new Chairman
(now in brand-new Armani) –
they're told, in no uncertain terms, to accept a pay freeze,
'as part of the measures required
to push through next year's business plan'.

No-one can quite believe it – the bare-faced cheek –
being told to accept, effectively, a pay-cut

from someone they know is making no such sacrifice.

But though everyone looks at him with daggers –

lightning daggers –

by the end of the meeting it's clear

that, this year,

a pay rise for anyone but the one in charge

is just as unlikely as lightning striking twice.

JACKPOT

Here I am at Oxford Circus station once again,
allowing myself to be part of the human jackpot
that's released each time a train pulls in.

I don't know if anyone else ever thinks this,
but whenever I'm on a train that's entering this station
and I'm watching the branded posters on the platform wall
whiz past my carriage window,
I'm reminded of playing a slot machine.

OK, this one has a single horizontal spinning drum
instead of the usual vertical three –
but it's not like the odds are stacked
any more in my favour.

The train's come to a stop,
and my carriage window reveals a mixed line:
Gap Kids, Nike Air, and the Oxford Circus roundel sign.

Whatever the combination though, I'll never win:
It's Oxford Street that always wins the prize…

…with today being no exception:

The carriage empties,

and every other carriage is emptying too,

as shoppers flow like coins from every exit of the train.

What else can we do at this stop,

when we've all been programmed since birth

to have nothing else but shopping on the brain?

INVISIBLE TWIN

I am a conjoined twin.

My other half is the invisible man.

We're joined at the hip.

Pretending to lean against an imaginary wall

is my party trick.

In any event, I'm required by law

to make any person I talk to fully aware

that my twin brother is also there, attached to me.

This relates to an apparently blank section

in the Mental Health Act,

which isn't blank at all but printed in invisible ink,

invisible to all but specialist lawyers

with their ultraviolet eyes and hidden fees.

But despite the fact that, in legal terms,

he's attached to me

(as opposed to me being attached to him),

it's my invisible brother who, relatively speaking, is free.

It's me who's imprisoned –

with all my 'profiles', 'cover pictures' and 'featured photos'.

Sometimes I wonder, is social media
simply the latest trick employed
to fool people into thinking
that they're always going to be visible,
and that, like religion, it's simply a trap?
Sooner or later, we'll all be hit by the terrible truth…

…that there really is nothing any of us can do
to avoid the same oblivion
that my invisible twin is forced to face up to everyday,
right from the moment he wakes up
or, indeed, is woken up, in the morning, by me,
anxiously tapping away on my phone,
already embarking on yet another daily round
of updating all my social media platforms –
one by one (then over and over again) –
desperately trying to remain in sight
and, as ever, desperately trying to ignore
the increasingly insistent tapping on my shoulder
from my peeved brother who wants nothing more
than to simply rest in peace.

NIGHTCLUBBING IN BRUM, 1988

I look a right sight

as I'm travelling into Brum on a Saturday night.

It's hard enough making the grade

when still a hapless teen at the tail end of Thatcher's decade,

and though one plus

about these times is that I'm able, still, to smoke a fag

while swigging a can of beer

on the top deck of the bus,

the biggest drag

is having to wear a suit –

it's taking the piss –

and I can't believe I'm saying this,

but it's lucky I chose branch banking as a career,

for it's 1988,

and though everyone says how much they hate

being made to wear a suit

(that's more often than not a Mr Byrite one to boot),

us fellas

have no choice but to dress

as if we've all got jobs

as bank tellers

just to get into nightclubs – in my case, one called fucking Snobs!

Who are we meant to impress

or even fool?

We're all still just a bunch of yobs –

just ones who don't look cool,

and there's fuck all we can do, for it's 1988,

and though everyone says how much they hate

being made to wear a suit

(that's more often than not a Mr Byrite one to boot),

rave ain't hit the mainstream yet

to liberate the dress code

and the Roses ain't made their boisterous baggy entrance yet

to liberate the playlist at Snobs from endless Depeche Mode,

the Blow Monkeys, Hue and Cry and fucking Lloyd Cole.

Well, one thing at least: I ain't still on the dole.

But, unfortunately, I work for a bank – Lloyds Bank.

I hate the job but it's them I have to thank

for payday,

and being as I don't just need this suit tonight but also on Monday,

I really oughta

drink less, not more,

or else by the end of the night,

I'll find I have a suit that's soiled with spilt Snakebite.

All I know is, whenever I dare to step onto Snobs' sunken dance
floor —
which is much like stepping into a paddling pool without water
(as it happens, I dance like a toddler in a paddling pool,
especially to 'Welcome to the Monkey House', the best ever song,
which turns me into a flailing fool,
a chimp in a suit) —
well, something usually ends up going wrong.

Last week, I tore my trousers and lost a button,
and being as I work for Lloyds Bank in Sutton
(high standards in that posh part of town),
I don't want yet another dressing down,
for it's 1988,
and though everyone says how much they hate
being made to wear a suit
(that's more often than not a Mr Byrite one to boot),
I at least get value out of mine,
but some consolation! – Roll on 1989...

JAN, JEN OR JEAN

I hadn't seen her in years.
Her name was Jan, Jen or Jean,
I couldn't remember which.

My face lit up like a fruit machine
when she caught my glance
as we passed each other on Southwark Bridge.

"Hi, Tom," she said,
and as if she'd pressed PLAY,
I felt compelled to take the chance.

The names began to spin inside my head –
Jan, Jen, Jean.
I pressed STOP too quickly –
I had little choice –
and settled on Jean.
"Hi, Jean," I said.

We passed.
I pressed COLLECT,
and got a sick feeling in my gut,

as the name Jan,

for first prize,

flashed before my eyes.

COMBATIVE

SHOPPING WITH PERSEUS

The night before I made my first daunting
solo shopping trip to Oxford Street,
Perseus appeared, in the dark, at the end of my bed.

He gave me such a fright but it was uncanny:
His tunic, sandals, curly hair and ruggedness
were exactly as depicted in the book
I'd studied that day in school.

He ordered me to sit up and listen carefully,
for he was here, he said,
to warn me about a new type of gorgon –
the "fashion victim" –
which lurked in every clothing store on Oxford Street.

"The fashion victim is hideous. Don't look directly at one.
Anyone who gazes into an undiscerning eye gets turned to plastic.
You must believe it. Where did you think
those showroom dummies come from?"

I was stunned by this revelation,
and Perseus, seeing he had my full attention, continued:

"Fashion victims can be recognised
by their permanently bulging eyes
caused by ridiculous prices on labels,
and the multi-coloured dreads which are actually snakes..."

With that, I immediately knew
that what he thought were gorgons
were simply people copying
the glamour-grebo style of the Kill Kids,
whose latest, and biggest, hit was "Snake Eyes",
and Perseus – having obviously seen the video,
in which their multi-coloured dreads
turn into snakes – had mistakenly thought
that what was simply fashion was a matter of life and death.

"Your mission is to enter their lair..."

"Their lair?"

"It's called Topshop:
locate and buy one pair of winged sandals
(make sure they're the red ones),
and then straightaway get out of there.
I would go myself, but I am three thousand years old,

far too old to get served in a place like that, but you are young.

Your lack of fashion sense has rendered you invisible,

there are mirrors everywhere to guide you

and your teenage habit of gazing at your shoes,

and never looking into peoples' eyes

when they talk to you nor you to them,

will hold you in good stead

when dealing with these creatures.

So go forth, and get me the winged sandals in red."

Well, I knew even then

that I wouldn't be able to find what he was looking for,

and the gorgons weren't actually gorgons.

But not wanting to make a three-thousand-year-old man feel bad,

I decided, the following night, when Perseus came to see me again

to ask me how my shopping trip had gone, to make up a story.

I told him I went into Topshop as instructed

(and onwards up to Topman)

and, when he asked *did the gorgons appear*,

I said no, as word had spread that a fearless human,

protected by Perseus and the Goddess Athena,

was on his way,

and they'd all be killed if they stuck around,

but, unfortunately, before the gorgons fled,

they destroyed all the stock in the winged sandals section,

and that's why I couldn't get my hands on a pair.

Perseus, though crestfallen, thankfully seemed to buy my story.

He said, don't worry about it...

...then asked me for one more favour:

Could I next week go instead to Gap

and get him a cap of invisibility?

SOCIALIST WORKERS ON OXFORD STREET

Even in front of Topshop,

entrenched behind a trestle table,

the Socialist Workers are unable

to make their presence felt.

They can't be missed – but the twist

is that it's not like they'd be missed,

these class warriors,

armed with four semi-automatic mouths

and a vast array of incendiary anti-capitalist texts,

who think that shoppers want to be liberated,

unable to see that shoppers, instead,

have turned their faces into impenetrable shields of apathy.

Sure enough,

when the fierce-looking man in the red shirt

yells out "Get yer Socialist Worker!", no-one does:

not one shopper shows the slightest interest,

not even a cursory sideways glance.

Even when the tiny but very loud woman

in the purple dress – with a voice as shrill

as the passing buses' screeching brakes –

screams "Capitalism kills!", the attack is again repulsed
by an endless sea of blank expressions.

Granted, the Socialist Workers are religious –
religious enough to keep on going through thick and thin –
whereas, me, I'm doubting Thomas, needing proof
and, unable now to get it, left with nothing;
and I don't know who's worse off.

In any event, I hate that everyone and everything
is threatened with being submerged
by what appears to be an unstoppable tide of commerce
and all that's left to confront it now
are four delusional Communist King Canutes.

STATEMENT BY THE PEDESTRIAN LIBERATION ORGANISATION

We, the PLO (Pedestrian Liberation Organisation),

do hereby swear, on the sacred Highway Code,

that those who dare to attempt to kill pedestrians as they cross the

road

will, from tomorrow, incur the deadly wrath of London's Shining

Path.

The revolution will not be televised – it will be pedestrianised –

and our enemies had better watch out.

White van man – each morning, for fun,

you try to run pedestrians over

at the zebra crossing at the start of Shaftsbury Avenue.

You arrogant sod: you need to know that what you do

will, tomorrow, be avenged by a PLO hit-squad.

Hippy cyclist – too busy having dreams

about saving the planet, it seems,

to think about pedestrians

when you jump the lights at Bishopsgate.

You're so into human rights,

except when it comes to people

travelling round London on foot.

Well, be left in no doubt:

tomorrow, the PLO will sort you out.

Bus driver – driving the 66 to Gants Hill,

like you're driving the 666 on the Highway to Hell,

getting a cheap thrill

out of beeping terrified pedestrians

as they try to cross New Wanstead.

You may be the Devil in a red bus,

but you need to know

that Hell hath no fury like avenging members of the PLO.

And black cab driver –

whose views and life story can't be ignored:

Your face, filled with malice,

when you deliberately try to mow down shoppers

crossing Westow Street in Crystal Palace,

equally can't be ignored.

No "knowledge" will help you tomorrow once the revolution's

underway,

when it won't be just the shoe on the other foot

but both shoes firmly on both feet,

not to push down any clutch or throttle

but to march along each street,

pedestrians no longer sheep penned on pavements –

bleating 'two legs good, two wheels bad, four wheels worse' –

but liberated lions roaring revolution,

making every vicious vehicle speeding down the road reverse.

We, the PLO (Pedestrian Liberation Organisation),

do hereby swear, on the sacred Highway Code,

that, from tomorrow, it will be so.

OBSOLETE

Ayatollah Khomeini's sermons on cassette tape,
smuggled into Iran
and copied over and over again,
fomented revolution.

To think, it was the cassette tape
that made powerful again an obsolete theology
and, not long after it did,
became an obsolete technology.

SAVAK couldn't compete with TDK
that couldn't compete with ARK
(Ayatollah Ruhollah Khomeini).

And now the Shia-inspired Islamic State he founded
is spreading its message via the internet
(its influence continuing to spread
as it fights – and defeats –
a Sunni-inspired Islamic State
that's also been spreading its message via the internet)
and one thing I've learned
is not to assume it will last,

that the internet, just like the cassette,

will undoubtedly soon be a thing of the past.

THE PHONEY WAR

Our imaginations at war –
with umbrellas for rifles,
our enemy invisible –
we defended the sofa,
had it pulled out from the wall.

Inside this narrow tunnel –
with seat cushions overhead –
we hid.

With each attack, we watched each other's backs.
You saw the Germans in your mind I could not see,
and I saw mine;
We shot them all too easily.

With the air-strikes, though,
we met our match.
Shells – like steel fists – struck,
and the seat cushions,
punched up into the air,
fell about us.

So, we rose and came out fighting –

shot down five fighters

and three bombers

with two umbrellas,

then finished off the conflict

in close hand-to-hand combat.

By the end,

there were a thousand German casualties

and, without even a scratch between them,

two tired Tommies,

smoking pencils, feeling tough.

And now the war was finished,

and with both of us famished,

we ran from the living room into the kitchen,

calling for Gran to serve us up our tea,

and found her quietly sobbing at the stove.

CORRUPTED

SAID CONTENTS

Parasite pocket

engulfs a paradise pocket

to snip its contents.

This time round,

to get said contents

without us even having to meet,

I scammed your cam,

got you naked on the first go –

the first fucking go.

A secret scam.

Keep it secret now, you hear?

Stay shtum,

and the scam stays secret.

You understand?

Just between you and me –

you and me only –

you snipped piece of pocket fabric.

Just let the pound coins –

those gold pound coins –

drip down your trouser leg like piss,

the last drops of piss you have,

drops as hard

as my hard heart,

piss turned to ice

like a Moscow-dreaming SS soldier's.

Can you see him now?

I can: He's just like you,

a teenage boy,

put out on guard duty,

pissing in the snow –

piss turning solid even as it flows.

No retreat, no advance.

It's a Siberian wind

for the gullible goose-step.

But that's how you are,

Mr. Teenage Western Man –

thinking you've got the whole world

at your fingertips

as soon as you've logged in.

That's the thing:

everyone thinks they rule the world

on the internet,

but all they do is get butt naked —
butt fucking naked.

And I whistled to you
through the hole in your cam,
but it was a keyhole I was blowing through,
entering your room
as easily as a ghost,
like a Siberian wind
now turning to ice
the conqueror's mind.

JUST ONE COMMA AWAY

I love throwing commas,

like daggers, into words.

Com,plete.

Fu,ll.

Blo,ck.

It kills them all stone dead.

Death is the great leveller.

Pap,er.

Sciss,ors.

Ro,ck.

The Rasputin of long words is

Supercalifragilisticexpialidocious.

It took seven commas to bring it down:

Supe,rcalif,ragi,listi,cexpi,alid,oci,ous.

The Education Secretary

has made a statement in the Commons

saying this makes no sense,

and that commas killing words

by splitting them

is no rule of grammar

which will ever be taught in schools.

But the Education Secretary

doesn't seem to get

that nothing makes sense anymore –

and now, with commas corrupted,

education, as we know it, is pointless

and just one comma away

from being brought down.

In fact, there's no point to anything anymore

except the one that's always there

at the end of a comma.

Let's face it,

now the rules have gone to hell,

and commas can kill,

there's no going back.

It's just another word

that's there to be brought down:

Ed,u,cat,io,n

IT WAS A CUT-UP

Even before police developed the first prototypes
of the stinger strip,
Mr Gysin and Mr Burroughs developed the cut-up.

Seeing the gas-guzzling car of the great American novel,
with its tyres of tradition
careering out of control before them,
Mr Burroughs threw the long, jumbled sentence of a cut-up
across the road,
causing the car to come to a grinding halt.

I guess you'd have to say it was Mr Burroughs' fault –
though of course he wasn't to know
how explosive the cut-up was
when it came into contact with tyres of tradition –
but the car blew up,
producing a fireball so huge,
it was even seen by Mr Calder in Britain.

But it wasn't a fuck up, it was a cut-up,
and Mr Burroughs stuck around
long enough for the fire to die down

and, from the burnt-out wreckage,

he pulled out the blackened corpse of the novel,

and with the help of his greatest character, Dr Benway

(who was armed only with a sink plunger

and a rusty pair of pliers),

the great American novel was somehow reanimated

and sent on its way, albeit undead

(at least it no longer had to pander to conservatives

but simply feed on their putrid brains instead).

HOOKED

It's mad to think
I'm just thirteen
and already hooked.

One moment of boredom
alone in the house
was all it took.

Imagine the best sneeze you've ever had,
then multiply it a thousand times
and still you're nowhere near
how good it felt.

I would never have believed
that one tablespoon of the stuff
could do so much.
All I can think about now
is the next score –
and who cares
that the real trouble begins
when you share your syringe
with others in relationships:

I'm in enough trouble already

with my suddenly-worsening grades at school,

but the problem is,

I just don't give a shit anymore.

Mrs Lane, our religious studies teacher,

told us all to Just Say No,

but little does she know

that she's the reason I started.

Most days I shoot up

in a cubicle

in the boys' toilet during break,

thinking of Mrs Lane

to heighten the pleasure

as the drug begins to hit.

It may be sleazy,

but what can I do?

And the teachers in the school

may disapprove –

but I can see,

in their junk-sick eyes,

that they're addicted too.

THE SURGERY I GO TO HAS A TWO-HEADED DOCTOR

The surgery I go to has a two-headed doctor.

'Doctor Smith will see you, see you, now.'

It gets very confusing.

Doctor Smith, via his left head,

gives me a diagnosis

then, via his right head,

gives me a second opinion,

which always differs from the first

(and that opinion's never the best one –

always the worst).

When Doctor Smith examines me with a stethoscope,

it's in the left head's left ear

and the right head's right ear.

In other words, he makes a right pig's ear

(and also a left pig's ear)

of any examination he does.

However, when I once challenged him about it,

Doctor Smith's left head simply said,

'Can you breathe in a bit more deeply, please?'
while his right head shook morosely.

Apparently, his wife has two heads as well,
and two pairs of breasts.
It's said they met as impoverished
but physically normal students,
earning money by undergoing laboratory tests.

Two heads are better than one, they say,
but I'm not too sure that comes into play
while attending an appointment with
the always-in-two-minds Doctor Smith.

FIRST KISS

Bone tongue

sticking out

of grinning knee,

a mouth

where it shouldn't be,

wet and pink

like a lizard's gawp,

a mean mimic

of the mouth

that's screaming into silence

the whole of the playground.

Fun fossilised

at the sight of bare bone,

the teachers keeping us back,

not wanting young children to see

an open-mouthed kiss

set in stone

at the exact moment,

after the knee

locked its non-existent lips

with the steps,

that those lips,

prized open,

came to be.

But I did see it,

unfortunately,

a gangly-gained gash,

extreme pornography,

a mouth

where it shouldn't be,

the first kiss

I remember most clearly.

LITERAL LIBRARY

In the local Literal Library,

under the section marked THE NAZIS,

there are hundreds of books by gay, Jewish and socialist authors

and, at the end of each shelf, a box of matches.

In the section marked ISLAM,

there are fifty copies of the Koran

and just one book of interpretation,

which changes frequently,

depending on which fundamentalist group has control of the shelf.

There's no longer any room for books which are off message

on the LIBERALISM shelf

which, unfortunately, has been taken over by hard-line fanatics.

Dwarfing all these sections

is a whole bay reserved for CAPITALISM –

shelves which are fully stocked,

though only with copies of a book entitled Choice.

So much Choice, but that's the thing:

No choice but Choice – and only one kind of Choice –

Choice but no choice.

Meanwhile, the bay beside it, marked COMMUNISM –

which collapsed many years ago – is yet to be repaired,

with the full extent of the damage hidden still

by life-size cardboard cut-outs of Kim Jong-un and Kim Jong-il.

And remaining rigidly in position –

therefore less obvious a wreck,

(but just as wrecked all the same) –

the half bay that's allocated

to THE ROMAN CATHOLIC CHURCH

has somehow ended up with multiple copies of

The Sex Guide for Lovers,

all of them masquerading as religious books,

with identikit pictures of the Pope on all the covers,

while the other half of the bay –

the half that THE ROMAN CATHOLIC CHURCH

looks down upon – ATHEISM, is completely and utterly empty

(only because the books have all been borrowed –

and in the Literal Library,

once a book is borrowed from that section, no record is kept).

AUTHOR BIOGRAPHY

Thomas McColl was born in 1970 and lives in London. He's had poems published in magazines such as Envoi, Iota, Prole, Riggwelter, Atrium, London Grip and Ink, Sweat & Tears, and his first collection of poetry, Being With Me Will Help You Learn, was published in 2016 by Listen Softly London Press. One of the poems from the book, The Chalk Fairy, was subsequently included in the Shoestring Press anthology, Poems for Jeremy Corbyn, and ended up getting quoted in the Evening Standard. He's read and performed his poetry at many events in London and beyond - including Celine's Salon, The Quiet Compere, Birkbeck Writer's Room and Newham Word Festival - and has been featured on East London Radio, Wandsworth Radio and TV's London Live.

ABOUT FLY ON THE WALL PRESS

A publisher with a conscience.
Publishing high quality anthologies on pressing issues, chapbooks and poetry products, from exceptional poets around the globe.
Founded in 2018 by founding editor, Isabelle Kenyon.

Other publications:
Please Hear What I'm Not Saying
(February 2018. Anthology, profits to Mind.)
Persona Non Grata
(October 2018. Anthology, profits to Shelter and Crisis Aid UK.)
Bad Mommy / Stay Mommy by Elisabeth Horan
The Woman With An Owl Tattoo by Anne Walsh Donnelly
the sea refuses no river by Bethany Rivers
White Light White Peak by Simon Corble
Second Life by Karl Tearney
The Dogs of Humanity by Colin Dardis
Small Press Publishing: The Dos and Don'ts by Isabelle Kenyon
Alcoholic Betty by Elisabeth Horan
Dinner In The Fields by Attracta Fahy
Awakening by Sam Love
House of Weeds by Amy Kean and Jack Wallington

Social Media:
@fly_press (Twitter)
@flyonthewall_poetry (Instagram)
@flyonthewallpoetry (Facebook)
www.flyonthewallpoetry.co.uk

More from Fly on the Wall Press...

Alcoholic Betty by Elisabeth Horan

ISBN10 1913211037
ISBN13 9781913211035

The brave and vulnerable poetry collection of Elisabeth Horan's past relationship with alcohol. Unflinchingly honest, Horan holds a light for those who feel they will not reach the other side of addiction.

"This is the hole. I go there
On Sundays. I go there after dinners
Before school --- mid work day
After lunch with the boss Mondays

The hole has Hangover coal
To paint my face to smudge
In the acne, rosacea, colloscum"

"Alcoholic Betty, we know the story. She died. Or did she? Through the "hours of penance" that is alcoholism and its attendant chaos-math and aftermaths, recurrent false dawns and falsetto damnations, Elisabeth Horan forges a descent/ascension pendulum of fire poems that are not "a map to martyrdom" - but a call to "go nuclear - Repose. Repose." Alcoholic Betty, we know the story. She died. She died so she could live."

- Miggy Angel, Poet, Author and Performer